The Entrepreneur's Handbook

Daniel Desta

DEDICATION

I would like to dedicate the creation of this book to my mother for being my number one fan in all of my crazy endeavors. Over a decade of good and bad decisions she has had the chance to see me at my very highest level of success to my very bottom of not being able to rub two nickels together. I have also had many people along my journey who have become family to me over the years.

Thank You all for all your support and I appreciate everything you all have taught me along the ways that made me who I am today.

CONTENTS

Introduction:

Congratulations on picking up The Entrepreneur's Handbook! I'm a firm believer that we can't win until we at minimum begin, and well, you've begun!

Now the question becomes: Why should you REALLY read this book, rather than just allowing it to collect dust? After all, let's be honest: For years you may have found yourself going back, and forth over tasks you've put off. Perhaps told yourself that you'd get to them all when you became more financially equipped, when the kids went off to college, or even the infamous: "I'll get to them all when I have time".

While this all may have sounded completely logical, the major problem therein lied in the fact that the perfect time to start may have never come. We ALL will inevitably meet road bumps, as well as challenges that can easily slow us down, or get in our way. What we must understand, and embrace is that the perfect circumstances, or outside sources were never required in order for us to begin. The perfect time to start, is always in your now. Look at it this way: The next five seconds in our lives aren't promised, let alone tomorrow.

Now I know it may sound crazy, but the truth is that your true calling in life has been embedded within you this entire time, and you've been fully equipped with nearly everything you need to see it to fruition. What tends to happen is when we allow distractions, or our fears to prevent us from beginning a journey on a road less traveled, we stay stagnant. We end up never beginning at all. We become discouraged by those road bumps, and challenges.

Sound a little familiar? The good news is that if it does, these experiences are what produce great character, and are very much what make you human. By now you may be toying with the idea of putting this book back on the shelf, or continuing to read on. I'm going to share some startling statistics with you in order to help your decision along:

1. Studies show that nearly 1/3 of high schooler's will not read another book after they graduate.

2. 42 percent of college students will never read a book after they graduate.

3. Finally 80 percent of U.S. families did not buy, or read a book in the year 2013.

As an author, one may think that these figures would have alarmed me, or even halted my decision to publish this book. That is quite the contrary! I realize that becoming an entrepreneur isn't FOR everyone, thus this message won't be received BY everyone. However, for the few that will receive this message, and thus become better because of it, THAT was motivation enough to put this book out!

Further, those road bumps, and challenges I mentioned earlier that we can't allow to stop us, also applies to the writer of this book. When we ALL see a road bump, or a challenge, WE must keep going.

You see, when you desire to live the life you've always wanted, you're going to find yourself not fitting under any statistical umbrella. Additionally, you'll find yourself pushing past limits, and tackling mountains that others haven't either wanted to climb, or just have plain old refused to climb.

If you've chosen to keep reading, I commend your decision! That is the first step to creating a better version of you, which in turn will create the better outcomes you have been searching for.

In this book you will learn how to push past the negative thoughts that limit your growth. You'll understand why fear has kept you from pursuing the goals you've always wanted. You'll also walk away with solid key principles that will ensure your success.

I've compiled some very real personal experiences along with every lesson I'll share. In other words, in order for this book to even exist, I had to live out each lesson first. I truly understand, and know this book will help you along your journey.

They often say that the best teachers learned from very real personal experiences. With that said, here is my personal story:

At the age of 18, I set out on a quest for a better future. Having decided to leave Devry University after just one semester, I packed my bags, and left Columbus, Ohio in pursuit of bigger, and better things. I knew there had to be something more in store for me.

With the reluctant blessing from my family who didn't quite agree with my decision, (they thought it was too risky at my age) I was on my way to California with nothing more than a book bag, and a dream.

Quickly finding my bearings, I settled in San Jose, California, and immediately made plans of action for my future. As fate would have it, I stumbled upon an ad in the paper that caught my attention. The ad read, "Looking for Loan officers. No experience needed! Will train! You can earn up to $10,000 a month!"

As one can imagine, this opportunity was much too good to pass up! I immediately made the call, and set up an interview.

Unbeknownst to me, that interview would change my life. The interview process in of itself was a bit more than what I expected. It was actually a group interview with twelve people in the room. Soon the President of the company walked in and stated that "of the twelve in this room, only one or two would be successful."

Of course, I was determined to be one of those two, and after just a couple months, I was the only loan officer left standing. By year number two, I had become a managing member of the firm and began to hire and train agents on my own.

By this time, life was honestly great! Here I was, 21 years old bringing in between 15-20K a month, and had just purchased my first home. This was unheard of at my age.

I was paying a mortgage of $4,998, driving a luxury car with a payment of $1876.00 a month, and living the high life. Needless to say, I didn't have anyone giving me solid counsel, or advice in reference to saving or investing my money.

Naturally, I did what most 21 year old's would've done. I blew through all of my money fast. I bought the most expensive things that I'd ever wanted. Paid for lavish expenses my new-found, "friends" had, and didn't plan for a rainy day. After-all, I thought this is what successful people were supposed to do, and didn't think a slow season would come---let alone a drought.

Here I was, thinking I'd finally made it......

The Great Recession in 2008 hit, and let's just say it hit me, and most people in the

United States like a ton of bricks! People lost jobs, families lost homes, and for me, I lost 88% of the revenue I was making. My mortgage had begun to pile up, and after so many calls from Mercedes, it was that time to return my car.

Again, I hadn't prepared for the worst. Never expected things could, or would change so rapidly for me. It was absolutely heart breaking interviewing for other jobs that would only pay me $2,500-$3,000 a month, when I was use to making ten times as much.

Of course the, "friends" that I acquired while I was making money were nowhere in sight when I could no longer cover the bill at the top nightclubs.

This was the point that I hit rock bottom.

I had to make a decision. I could either settle for a basic job just getting by, or I could be innovative. Early on, I developed my own guiding principle. That principle? "Where there is a will, there is always a way", and that carried me through my rough time. I tapped into my inner-self, and drew from all the things I had been equipped with to create. It was at this pivotal moment that an Entrepreneur was born.

I saw past my rough patch, and instead saw opportunity. I put my entrepreneurial spirit to work, and founded Funding International Exchange, a company that provided privatized funding for major commercial developments.

After starting my firm, I reached out to some of the wealthiest firms, families, and fellow entrepreneurs offering them the chance to invest in various projects, and promising them a healthy return on their investment.

This networking paid off, and soon clients came to realize that I was operating with a unique business model. I had created a streamlined process of investing, which made it easier for clients to make clear decisions.

With my success in helping clients invest wisely, and then subsequently seeing a return on those investments, I next turned my attention to helping start-up entrepreneurs and small business owners. After-all, I could relate to my clientele very well, as I had once been there. Through my experiences, "The Entrepreneur's Handbook" was birthed. I invite you to read, enjoy, and process all the information, and lessons that you'll take away.

Let's begin.

CHAPTER *1*
Identifying Your, "WHY?"

*W*hen you wake up every morning, WHY have you decided to move forward in your day? What is your driving force? This chapter will not only help you identify your own personal why, but it will also teach you how to stay encouraged when those closest to you, may not back you.

Often times when entrepreneurs choose to chase their dreams instead of working a, "realistic/normal 9-5 job", they are smacked in the face with everyone asking them, "*Why?*"

Why would you knowingly work a, "job" that is going to be uncertain financially, more than likely will offer no benefits, no retirement plans, and is all the round seemingly unstable? Their questions while annoying and even possibly damaging are actually quite normal! All that you've decided to willingly go up against is absolutely going to seem absurd to those that aren't doing it!

You've got to remember that not everyone has been built to be an entrepreneur. Therefore, this line of work is not going to be for, or supported by everyone. Remember: Do NOT take their lack of understanding, or questioning personal. There, "why" is going to be completely different from yours! As a result, they're not going to always understand your drive. Your risk taking. Your processing.

In the beginning of an entrepreneur's journey their "why?" is typically relatively easy to answer. They've come up with an innovative idea that they believe they're going to make a great living with.

They believe their lives will change for the better because of it. This is all very reasonable! After all, who would willingly start a business knowing for a fact they'd fail? Businesses are generally started because success feels very attainable.

Soon thereafter however, reality starts to settle in. All of the sacrificed time, energy, and resources that starting the business, program, organization, or project is going to take can feel quite daunting.

Further, when the money doesn't roll in at the pace one expected, and the debt begins to pile up, it becomes harder and harder for the said entrepreneur to believe in their "why?"

Eventually they start asking themselves not only the same questions that their critics asked, but some additional:

"Why am I doing this again?"

"Why am I putting my lively hood at risk?"

"Why am I risking my relationships?"

"Why am I knowingly plummeting myself head first into debt?"

"Why am I doing something that is inevitably going to bring me stress and anxiety?"

The truth is, these questions are also very normal, and go through most entrepreneur's minds at least once. Stress tends to produce doubt. Doubt tends to produce fear, and makes one re-think the whole "innovative idea", they once passionately believed in.

This is the fork in the road separating those who know that if the pursuing of one's dreams were easy, the whole world would be filled with startup businesses. Innovative ideas floating everywhere.

As I mentioned earlier, inevitably there are going to be those who don't, or won't understand entrepreneurship. Those who aren't mentally prepared to face the challenges ahead because they're either so accustomed to playing it safe, were burned in the past when taking risks, or finally, they've lived a life so full of struggle, that they aren't willing to put their livelihood at risk again.

The consistent idea to keep in mind, is that the passion, and purpose that you have belongs to YOU. Not everyone is going to understand, or support you.

Additionally, understand that your, "why" shouldn't solely be attached to money. Don't get me wrong---the goal is to indeed make a profit, but your why, should be attached/defined by your passion.

In other words, when you wake up, you decide to put in the work for the day because you KNOW with everything you have, this is what you were meant to do. Everything else that falls under that umbrella is an added bonus---in other words: Making money.

Now, some of you may feel that, "the reason why I do what I do, is to make money. Period. Passions don't pay. Work does." There's no denying that hard work is key. However, in order to get to the root reason of why you started is directly connected to your passion/purpose.

To start, ask yourself these questions, and be VERY honest with your answers. Why are you getting up every day? What is driving you? Why are you pressing forward? I've included hints below, but answers to your previous, "whys?" as well:

1. Why am I doing this again?

You have a strong belief system in your passion. You believe in your business, innovative idea, and/or movement. Your, "Why" quite simply is part of a deep strong belief system within yourself. It keeps you up at night. You think about pursuing it all the time. You have an unfailing belief that this will work.

2. Why am I putting my livelihood at risk?

You've decided to risk your lively hood because you understand that if there is no risk, there is no reward. This is why SO many people take the easy road! While many inhabit an entrepreneurial spirit, they still aren't quite grasping the concept that: Until you want to succeed as bad as you want to breath, NOTHING WILL BE EASY.

Think of the movie: "Pursuit of Happiness" as an illustrative example. This was an awesome biographical drama film based on entrepreneur Chris Gardner's nearly one-year struggle with homelessness.

It details his struggles as an entrepreneur, and shows the viewer that this individual held on to a belief system so strong, he risked it all only to later own a multi-million dollar brokerage firm.

While, "risking it all" may not be our desired path, his story gives us a prime example of an individual who not only knew their why, but was so firmly committed to it, that they refused to give up.

3.Why am I risking my relationships?

You decide to risk your relationships because you understand that the right people will be left standing by you, supporting you, and pushing you throughout the process.

You know that not everyone attached to you is going to advocate for what you're doing--- especially if the possibility of your income fluctuating/declining will affect them.

Another great example that supports this point:

Stephen King's first book published, "Carrie", was rejected more than thirty times leaving him defeated. While returning home with yet another refusal, he decided to throw his book in the trash. Later his wife came across it, and promptly fished it out.

While many around him didn't support what they thought was foolish, she insisted he try again. She understood, and supported his, Why. Standing by his side, she watched him sell close to 350 million copies of the very same book he'd thrown away.

4. Why am I knowingly plummeting myself head first into debt?

While you haven't actually decided to, "plummet deeply into debt", you personally understand the risks of entrepreneurship.

What is interesting is that debt is something people so easily accept in terms of a house, car, education, midlife crisis, etc., but it seems so hard for them to accept the idea that as an entrepreneur, it's going to take capital. Often, that capital being your own!

Here we see again:

Walt Disney's first animation company went bankrupt. It then motivated him to find financial funding for his project, only to be rejected more than 300 times when he tried to file for financial assistance. Today he's worth approximately 35 billion today.

5. Why am I doing something that is inevitably going to bring me stress and anxiety?

See answer number one before continuing.

Stress and anxiety are only momentary emotions, that aren't always negative.

Don't believe me? Flip on a good song, receive good news, or enjoy some type of endorphin producing food, and all of a sudden that feeling is gone. In relation to your business, stress, and anxiety typically indicates that you're not only passionate about what you're doing, but you care.

You see, when you care about something deeply, those emotions come just as naturally as happiness and contentment. Emotions are constantly in-motion!

In other words they are the indicators that something of meaning and great worth in our life is causing us, joy, pain, love, anger, stress, peacefulness, and the list goes on and on.

The key and not so easy piece is understanding that while your emotions aren't a bad thing, we don't want to allow them to override our intellect in business. In other words, you receive bad news, and make a bad decision. Good news produces a feel good decision. Stay away from this space!

The idea is to recycle any negative energy into fuel that will not only keep us going, but will also make us better.

So you see, one could ramble off a million reasons "why" you are continuing down a path so blatantly treacherous with just hopes of touching infinity.

However, none of them will be as definitive as the admittance that you are continuing on, because you understand that life is too short to be making other people's entrepreneurial ambitions, and dreams a reality.

You understand that it is YOUR time. You understand the importance of laying the bricks down for your own castle.

When others question an entrepreneur's "why", they don't realize they're questioning their very existence. It's already difficult living in a society where the very admittance that your, "why?" is actually a, "who?" and the, "who?"
just happens to be, "you".

If you are brave enough to admit out loud that your why is you, the wrong people are more likely to strike you down, rather than picking you up. Remember, they aren't supposed to necessarily understand, even though support is expected.

The wrong people begin greedily tapping their fingers waiting for the first signs of struggle so they can point and scream, "I told you so!" Or, "I knew starting your own business was a bad idea".

Little do they know, you have chosen this "treacherous" path. You have battled your inner fear. You have stood and faced emotions that once made you feel so small, or so insignificant that the only place to go was up.

In order to succeed, first you may have to fail, and to fail you have to be willing to let yourself, and everything else in your world fall. Trust the process.

You will be amazed to find that through this time in your life, the negative bits, and pieces from your being will begin to fall away. A much needed shedding will take place. What is uncovered is your drive. A drive that others may have looked at as irrational, or asinine.

Now then, are you ready to admit that your "why" is actually a "you"? In other words, YOU are your company. The passion embedded within YOU is there because YOU are the one to see it through. While our businesses are an extension of us, our passion, and inner being go hand in hand.

When you're ready to embrace this, that is when you will see that all those pieces that have fallen away, were for you to simply be reborn. Reprogrammed. Renewed.
Now, with the ability to accept success under all the pretenses, you're fully equipped, and ready, as you trusted the process. You understood, and believed in your why. Your why, meaning---YOU.

Feel free to re-read this chapter again as needed.

CHAPTER 2
Facing Your Fears and Coming Out on the Other Side

*F*ear, it is a simple word that represents a complex set of emotional, physical and chemical reactions in the human body. Our perception of the world around us and the way that we interact with that world can be made better, or worse by the way that we handle our fears.

Fear can be looked at as a base motivator for the majority of the human condition. For instance, It is fear of death, and fear of discomfort that causes us to work, and strive forward. It is the reaction that can keep us OUT of danger, and REMOVE us from danger if we find ourselves in the wrong situation. However, this natural reaction to the environment often grows out of control, and can alter our lives and ultimately our happiness.

Most entrepreneurs face two fears. The fear of rejection, and the fear of failure. When you begin to identify where these fears originate from, you soon separate yourself from the other entrepreneurs that are letting their fears consume them. Studies have also shown that entrepreneur's that operate in a space of fearlessness, have a higher chance of success than others that did not face their inner fears.

The Past

Many of our fears are based on one single experience, or a compilation of negative experiences from our past. Our mind consistently tries to create a template for happiness, and it is based upon what made us happy in the past. It is also based upon the avoidance of past situations that have hurt us physically, or emotionally.

This is a highly logical system that has been constructed around our perceptions. However, the problem with logic is that it is not accurate when it comes to dealing with other humans.

The mixture of the logic systems of two separate humans can create more confusion than it will alleviate. The other problem is that we rarely have exacting control over the way that this logic is created. We can tell ourselves time and time again that we are behaving in a manner that is not healthy and yet our base motivators do not change.

We've got to be willing to get out of the way of our own selves. The very fears that while are very much so real to us, are also a self-made road block that stunts our growth, and ultimately our success. We can all push past fears, but the reality is all of us won't. The fact that you're even reading this book, suggests that you're ready to put those fears aside, and catapult to your next level. Congrats again!

Past Interactions

We've all been hurt in some capacity. It's what makes us human. We've been on the receiving of emotional pain, or we've purposefully/inadvertently been the giver. The fact of the matter is, relationships are the bread and butter of our emotional well-being. Unfortunately, most relationships are prone to some pretty heavy damage.
Even in the presence of "unconditional love," we will find ourselves altering the way that we deal with future people in our lives, and

13

further alter the way we feel about those said people based on pain from the past.

The term "failed relationship" has a negative connotation around it. I've always been a fan of calling them, "learning experiences", instead. However, the truth of the matter is that often the "learning" process can cause us to draw more, "learning experiences" in the future if we never truly got through the first process. As an example, one simple three month relationship in high school can affect all subsequent relationships to follow.

Without following modern psychology, and the trend to go all the way back to the relationship with the parents, we can use this first relationship to see how it affects the future. The way that the relationship ended, and the events right before that moment will have a lasting effect on the future. Example: A woman that was "dumped" right before the senior prom can develop strange ideas about herself, and the future. She may begin to second guess her worth, her decisions, and her adequacy.

Most times, the other party will rarely be transparent about why they're ending the relationship and as a result, our perceptions will no doubt begin to create fear. Anyone that has been emotionally wounded by a breakup will inevitably develop a set of fear like responses that can alter their future if they let them.

Practice Makes Perfect

How does this relate to you, as an entrepreneur? Remember, in order to be successful at whatever you do, you've got to make certain that your mind is in the right place. Your past, "learning experiences/failed relationships", may cause you to treat your partners, employees, or even clientele a certain way based on what you've not dealt with. It's very human, but there's always an opportunity to be better.

Repeated breakups can start to set a trend in the mind of any entrepreneur. They will in the back of their mind start to create fear based patterns to avoid emotional pain in the future. Example: The first 30 seconds of a conversation with the opposite sex, or with someone that looks similar to whom you used to date, can possibly be forever changed based upon the past. This in turn, hurts them when making business decisions for a company, as they're now operating from an emotional place.

When our emotions start to override our intellect, this halts great business decisions. There may be the over eager person that is determined to let the past die, and is too forceful in pursuing the next relationship or business venture. Additionally, there may be the person that is far too shy, thus misses a chance at a great business venture because they are afraid of rejection. They take a decline of services, personally.

As another example: If we've ever encountered discrimination, which may, or may not influence how we view others we encounter that may have looked like the perpetrator. If we allow the recorded negativity in our memory to shape our reactions, then ultimately our maximum potential will stay out of reach.

Here's a final scenario: When a woman tells a man that she saw a job opening at her company that he fits the qualifications for, she may be trying to create more time to spend with him. If he allowed his past experience of a woman calling him a deadbeat to get in the way, he may lash out at his current Love.

On the flip side, a man that tells a woman that she has pretty eyes is not necessarily trying to get her in bed and leave her, no matter how many times that has happened to her in the past.

This is a very important point that I don't want you to miss, hence all of the examples. As we can see, fear is ultimately detrimental to our success personally, and professionally. As an entrepreneur, the two go hand in hand. YOU are the company, YOU are the brand. It is unfair to YOU and your consumer if you're tying in your past to your business processes.

The key is going to be to practice facing your fears, and to respond to what is real. NOT your perceptions. It is important to not overreact to any given stimulus. Remember, be open. Understand that not everyone is a shark out here to hurt you. When you expect all experiences to be the same, you are willfully setting yourself up for failure, and blocking progression. Faith, and fear cannot co-exist; they're like oil, and water. Surpass your fear---DO NOT let it surpass you.

Base of Fear

The Buddhist Monks have a saying about meditation. It is said to place yourself in the most uncomfortable situation, and remain there until it no longer hurts. Drug and alcohol recovery programs stress to not have a major relationship in the first year. It is only when we find ourselves face to face with our fears that we realize that there was not that much to fear in the first place.

Everyone will pass away one day. That is likely the biggest fear of all, yet it is the one thing that cannot be avoided at all. Accepting this fact, and accepting the fact that we'll inevitably be hurt, or disappointed in the future pushes fear aside. It isn't that you're walking around, and *waiting* for the inevitable to happen, but rather you're at peace with the road bump like circumstance.

Our lives are simply a set of experiences and the good; always make way for the bad. Our lonely days, and nights set the stage for the moment when our life is filled with another person. The cold winter days make it ever more pleasant to lie on the beach in the summer. Facing our fears, and realizing that it is simply not going to be as bad as we think, will open the door for new experiences in the future.

Like most, I personally had a terrifying fear of heights. I'd go to meetings in high rise buildings, and couldn't bear to go near the windows to look at the great views because in my mind, there was this impending danger. So, all those years I missed out on viewing beautiful scenery, because of a fear I made up in my mind. Honestly, my fear had no merit. I'd never fallen out of a building, so where was this coming from?

It wasn't until I began looking into how my fear of heights originated that things began to get puzzling for me. As a child, I would always jump from one tree to the next all the while being 7 feet off the ground. I fearlessly climbed houses, and jumped some feet to get down from them. So, at what point did things change?

One day, I got tired of having this phobia, and started to dig deeper. I truly wanted to see just where this fear originated from. That's when it hit me. When I became a teenager, I allowed the media to embed fear into my mind. I'd watch stories, and listen to facts of how athletes, and other people died from falling down the stairs, from a ladder while putting up Christmas lights, and a host of other scenarios. Overtime, fear quite naturally settled in.

After identifying where the fear came from, I made a plan of action to face each fear one at a time. This was a long, brutal process for me, but so well worth. I started out by learning the art of meditation to calm my mind, and silence the voice of fear within me.

Next, I made a, "Fear Bucket List". In other words, I wrote out a list of all the things I was afraid to do.

Zip Lining, was at the top of my list as I'd always had the thought that the line would most certainly break, and I'd meet my death. I wasn't playing when I decided to face this phobia! I reached out to all my adventurous type friends, as I didn't want to be discouraged, but rather encouraged.

As I rode in the backseat on the hour long ride to the location, I had plenty of time to meditate, and quiet my mind. When we arrived, I was actually more excited about doing it, as well as the rush it would provide. I was READY to conquer. To move forward. I was also eager to see how this would translate into other facets of my life.

After receiving the instructions, and precautions from the head facilitator, I was ready to get locked in. Armed with all the pertinent information, and now strapped in my harness, I walked up to the first line to hook onto. My friends insisted I go first, as they all knew how monumental this would be for me.

Here I am, finally hooked to the line that hopefully would carry me to the other side. I was finally tackling one of my first Fear Bucket List goals. I refused to look down, as I was truly looking forward literally and figuratively to reaching the other side.

Faintly I heard, "3, 2, 1," and finally I felt myself take off. Feeling the cool breeze of the beautiful forest, embracing the animals below, and flying over the lake, I felt like I went to Heaven. I finally had done what I set out to do, and realized I wasn't missing danger; I was missing the opportunity to live!

What I was afraid of ended up being one of my best experiences that I didn't want to end. By the time I got to the end of the line, all I could say was, "Let's go again!" From that point forward, I vowed to not allow my fears to hold me back again.

After the Zip Lining experience, I went on to sky diving, White water rafting, snowboarding, visiting the top of the Sears Tower in Chicago, as well as many other activities that allowed me to push past fear. Had I never took it upon myself to face the fears within; I wouldn't have been able to grow. Further, I wouldn't be able to share with you all the importance of facing your fears from a place of experience. I KNOW this way of life works, because I've lived it first.

It is fear itself that will ultimately hold you back from ever meeting your greatest potential within yourself. Be held back, no longer. Take your own limits off, and operate from a fearless place.

You'll not only grow leaps, and bounds, but so will everything around you. In other words, your business!

CHAPTER 3
Understanding Your Purpose in Life and Being Okay With It

*W*e all have a purpose/mission/assignment in life – whether it is to be a CEO, a parent, an entrepreneur, a famous musician, or a renowned leader to others. Some of us may not know our purpose in life until it hits us smack in the face, while others have known for as long as they can remember. Either situation is fine, and perfectly normal. The goal is that once you know your purpose, you accept, and embrace it.

In other words, if you've been called to be a baker, but you choose to become a pilot, you're out of alignment with that purpose. Confused with why you're not excelling, or at peace with what you're doing often leads back to the question: Are you working in your true purpose? It may turn out not to be what you planned for your life, but it may be exactly what you NEED to prosper and be happy with yourself.

If you never take a chance and go for your dreams, you will never know how successful you could've been. Imagine if Justin Timberlake had never decided to walk out his purpose of being a singer, or if Steve Jobs had never looked fear in the face, and didn't decide to go for it with Apple, or even if the great mothers and fathers of the world had decided it wasn't worth it. The world would be a much different place if not for people understanding their purpose in life, and walking it out!

Now, understand that it isn't always going to be easy to follow your dreams and purpose in life. It may mean years of struggle, heartbreak, or living an entirely different life than the one you imagined for yourself. It isn't necessarily easy, but all this can be worth it.

I never imagined my purpose in life to be what it is today. When I was a child, I had dreams of being a high-powered attorney like Johnnie Cochran. I watched him cover the O.J. Simpson trial amongst other high-profile cases. I had dreams of making it big solely for Daniel Desta---certainly not helping other business owners. I was trying to fit squares into circles, and wasn't as fruitful as I could have been.

As another example, I had a friend who went on a journey to find her true purpose in life. She had grown up wanting to be a sports journalist, but eventually found her way into a newsroom. She spent time studying, and working as a producer at multiple television news stations.

For that decade, she truly thought that was her purpose in life, and what she would be doing for years, and years to come. However, as her first son got a little older, she realized a much different purpose in life.

She had loved being a mother, but had never even considered being a stay-at-home mom until that point. Working outside the home was something she always expected to do. It still took more time to accomplish her goal, but now she is a stay-at-home mom to her two boys. It wasn't the glamorous life she planned out, but being real about her purpose, awarded her true happiness.

That friend got her chance to realize her purpose in life after her husband made a career change----he also had discovered his purpose! They completely downsized from their old life, but she realized she was at peace with this. Now, she is fulfilling her purpose in life, and couldn't be happier – despite the struggles that come with embracing the new direction.

I also had the pleasure to work with a man who had known exactly what his purpose in life was from the time he was young. He started working toward his goals as soon as he was allowed to enter the workforce. Yes, he had a daughter and was a good father, but his true calling and purpose in this life was in his work discipline.

He embraced the fact that it wouldn't always be easy – and in fact was going to be a struggle. He worked through years of making no money at a job he loved. Working up through the ranks, he now has a dream position in his industry. Of course, this would never have been attained if he hadn't been in acceptance of his purpose.

There is one particular person in my life that has probably one of the most difficult purposes I know. Her purpose is to help the less fortunate. I say it is difficult, because it is something that many won't do, nor even consider. She has been criticized for reaching out to the homeless, and substance abusers, warned about her potential safety being in jeopardy. Her response? That she has nothing to lose.

She lost her son to a debilitating disease a couple of years ago, and she isn't married. Her goal in life is to sow back into others when she can. Additionally, she doesn't have much money. More often than not, she makes just enough to get by.

Even so, I have seen her sit down for a meal with multiple homeless men, and women on a weekly basis. She brings them clothes, offers her phone for use to call family members, and has given rides to countless people as a way to help them get to a job interview.

She truly cares, and without her acceptance of a purpose that is quite heavy for most, dozens of people wouldn't have been impacted the way she has impacted them.

This leads us to entrepreneurship. If this is your true purpose, you'll know it, and will eventually see fruit from being in agreement with it. Being okay with it.

So, embrace your purpose in life – no matter what it is. You CAN be that head chef or Olympian. You CAN change the lives of others every day. You just have to realize your personal talents, and drive – and then go for it. Be okay with whatever you are truly here to do. Don't let the struggles, and road bumps of your journey stop you from success. Put your stamp on this world and make it a better place for everyone.

Here are 3 questions you must ask yourself, and of course be honest in answering:

- What is something that you can do that is effortless for you, but difficult for others?

- What would it take to turn that into a profession?

- What do you need to do to be satisfied with that?

Identify your answers, and then make a plan of action to get there.

CHAPTER *4*
Learning To Be Authentic With What You Do

*I*n a seminar I attended about being an entrepreneur, the speaker used the analogy that being an entrepreneur, is like *"having a chronic condition that lasts a lifetime."* In other words, once you become one, you're never cured. It is a, "condition" that the entrepreneur has to then learn to manage, for it cannot get out of his/her system.

I found this quote so very powerful, and it inspired me to offer a chapter on authenticity.

You see, there are those that either, "decide" to become an entrepreneur, or those that accept that this is what they were meant to do.

For those that have just, "decided" to walk this path, they're falling out of alignment with authenticity. It wasn't something that was embedded within them, and thus they never could really feel settled with the idea. Comfortable. At home.

The art of living authentically is when you choose to truly be yourself, flaws and all. When you live authentically personally, this approach can easily be carried over into your business. If you continuously paint the picture that everything is always peachy clean, it will become increasingly difficult for your followers/consumers to connect with you.

With every business there is an upside and a downside to it, which in turn makes your business real. Believe it or not, it is the faults that your consumers will be able to relate to in your business, thus turning into faithful clientele.

Truth is, people in today's society love a comeback story! When you can show how your business has improved, via lessons that have been applied from mistakes, it shows that the entrepreneur is always willing to change a few things to make the experience that much better for the consumer. You've seen the signs, "Pardon our dust", "Under new management", or "We're currently updating our services". This is a perfect example of a business that isn't hiding their growth process-----and as a result, customers often connect easier.

Maintaining authenticity is an easier said than done act as one ventures deep into their businesses. I say this because many business ventures start from a humble beginning but may reach massive success with time. It is important to not only maintain authenticity, but humbleness throughout the entire journey. You, your business, and client will all benefit because of your way of thinking.

Remember to maintain your authenticity, as it is the one thing that offers you an edge over your competitors in the market. It makes YOUR business unique. Yes, you may have been inspired by your competitors, but your business has YOUR own signature flowing all through it. Stay passionate about what you decide to do, and keep what has been embedded within you for the business close to your heart.

This is a direct advantage for you, as you'll find that running your business will feel effortless, and you won't be tempted to change your own style, to conform to the masses. Understand this: Customers and clients, who buy into your idea, do so because it is unique in its own way.

If you change it to match those of other people, your business not only runs the danger of losing its market share, but also your stamp on it.

When you decide to become an entrepreneur, it is important that you recognize the challenges that are ahead of you. I've lightly touched upon those challenges thus far, and will even more throughout this book.

The point is, is when you understand what you're up against, it allows you to devise your plan to keep pushing forward despite those said challenges. You won't give up before you reached your maximum potential, because of the stress the challenges brought forth.

Equipped, and ready, you'll find it easier to stay on the path that has been embedded within you, thus remaining in that authentic, true place. Remember your why, is YOU. You're worth staying committed, and true to you. All of the preparations and positive work you'll do will pay off on all levels.

Remaining in this authentic place, will allow you to be able to bring change to the industry or area that you desire to venture into. Your innovative idea, will challenge the status quo, and thus lead to an improved customer experience as you'll be able to provide them with an alternative to what has been previously in the market.

Having a sole set focus and targets to achieve with your business would also help you in maintaining your market share----*(the percentage of an industry or market's total sales that is earned by a particular company over a specified time period. Market share is calculated by taking the company's sales over the period and dividing it by the total sales of the industry over the same period.)*

When an entrepreneur has set targets, they work at perfecting their business ideas in order to achieve them, and maintain them well. These two qualities are very important for an entrepreneur as they act as the checks toward maintaining their authenticity in business.

A great example of a person who believes in being authentic in all you do is Philip Lett, the CEO of the Blur Group. He decided to create the concept of the Blur Group from his own vision and not only considered the profits he would receive but also the core values of the company. He wanted to create a disruptive force in the market as he believed that it would bring about a change to the various industries he had worked with in the past.

Lett claims that the only piece of advice he may offer to any budding entrepreneur would be for them to think long, and hard about what it is they want out of life, as well as from the business they want to venture into. After setting clear goals, it is his opinion that they'll be able to remain true to their selves and also to their idea. His company has been successful due to his belief of being authentic in whatever you do.

So, as we see, authenticity works in all facets. Remain true to who you are personally, and professionally. Life and business flows easier by remaining in that space.

CHAPTER 5
Branding 101

The overall success of your business depends on having a solid brand that customers can buy into. Branding involves so much more than just choosing the right company name, and logo. It's all about building trust, creating the right image, and owning a business that is seen as being consistent.

Think about it this way: When you make the choice to buy a car, typically there are certain desired brands that come to mind. Even when ordering a glass of wine, you may not necessarily be thinking of the cheapest wine, but rather the wine you KNOW will taste good. The branding is embedded in the mind. Most consumer decisions are based on how a brand is generally perceived, and on the reputation it has gained.

Public perception of a brand does not just depend on aggressive marketing, or an extensive advertising campaign. It relies much more on building trust, which can only come from brand awareness, word-of-mouth recommendation, product placement, and association with quality.

It is not enough just to advertise what a business has to offer. Branding will show how a product or service is different from similar ones in the same market. It is branding that will bring success, or failure to the business. Even an excellent product or service can fail when branding is not established, and the general impression is of something no one actually needs.

In order to establish a solid brand, it is necessary for an entrepreneur to consider such things as the tidy appearance of company premises, and the quality of website design. Branding also depends on how well business owners, and employees interact with customers. How was the customer treated face-to-face, and over the phone? Further, how long did it take the business to respond to inquiries, or issues?

Business correspondence and e-mails also play an important part of branding. An e-mail that is full of typing errors, poor grammar, incorrect spelling and badly worded phrases gives a negative impression, and will get only the briefest glance before it is trashed.

Branding a business also requires the owner to make sure it gains a good reputation through social media. The time it takes to respond, and the regularity of social media updates, can play a big part in building a reputation online.

A solid brand will always deliver exactly what is expected of it by consumers. Good customer service can go beyond the expectations of the average consumer, but customers should never receive anything less than they would expect from a solid brand.

From the 1950s through the 1980s, success in American business was dictated based on "what you knew" as a professional. In the dot.com era, success was typically driven by "who you knew." Starting with this new decade of 2010-2020, guaranteed success will be driven by "who knows you." Investing in marketing programs that establish YOUR BUSINESS as the most recognized in your market, and industry will propel your business forward.

Apple is a good example of a solid brand, because of its association with fast-paced technology, and constant innovation. Its products always provide exciting new features, and applications we want to use as soon as a new one is released. The company has gained many loyal customers because it is a brand that leads people to expect quality products which are easy to use, at a price they can afford.

Another example of a solid brand is not a corporation, it is an individual. Warren Buffet has established his own brand as a highly regarded self-made billionaire and investment guru. He started as an entrepreneur at the age of 13. By the age of 20, he had already earned 10,000----a considerable amount in 1950. His main product now is expert knowledge and sound financial advice.

Entrepreneurs who do not understand the importance of branding fail to build on their own reputation. Even a successful business will lose money when it is not a solid brand, and its customers will inevitably turn to other brands.

In 1954, Jack Tramiel, a New York taxi driver who also repaired typewriters for a living, founded the Commodore Portable Typewriter Company. By the 1980s Commodore was a top name in home computers, however the company went bankrupt in 1994. By then it had become uncompetitive, and had lost its focus. The business was finally associated with only offering outdated technology.

While expansion is important for keeping a brand at the top of the market, brand extension has also been the cause of product failure. An established brand must stick with products that appeal to its customers.

I have also known entrepreneurs that failed because they tried to create a brand that offered too many types of products or services. A business can only be a market leader when it specializes in one particular market, and is known for serving a specific market.

As an example, when a range of perfumes was introduced under the logo of Harley Davidson, the successful motorbike manufacturer had no success with that particular brand extension. It failed because the company brought out a product that was of little interest to the majority of motorcyclists who formed its loyal customer base.

Anyone who is not convinced about the power of branding should consider the following statistics:

*A strong brand image can boost a selling price by between 5 percent and 7 percent.

*62 percent of consumers have negative feelings about advertising and take more notice of product reviews.

*75 percent of consumer purchases are based purely on emotion, not on marketing messages.

*80 percent of revenue generated by a niche business will come from 20 percent of its customers.

The most important point to remember is that a solid brand is built up through trust, and it will remain a solid brand by staying consistent.

CHAPTER 6
How to Compete With the Giants

*T*he Internet has forever altered the way business is done domestically, and internationally. The global market has made companies like Amazon the most popular book store in the world while companies such as Barnes & Noble struggle to keep their heads above water. Fortunately small business owners, taking advantage of the monumental shift in the way business is done has never been easier.

Personally, one of the best ways my small company has become more competitive is by taking advantage of a strategy known as Search Engine Optimization (SEO). Like most small-business owners, I quickly realized the importance of having a website.

My company lends to small businesses in the state of Florida, and unfortunately, when I entered a query into any search engine, my office didn't even show up in the first 50 results. In fact, some firms were coming up two, and three times before mine.

After doing some research, I came across some information on SEO and came to the conclusion that I'd have to invest in this process if I was going to be successful.

After consulting with several firms, I decided to patronize another small company composed of college students who helped me understand the intricate details of this process. What happens is, search engines like Google have a certain criteria they consider when they rank the search results. This is why certain companies had their website appear two, or even three times before mine in the results because they'd already invested in SEO.

Since I used a local company, the service was pretty affordable but the next few days were particularly nerve wrecking. Though I hadn't spent a terrible amount to have the SEO done, I didn't have money to waste on a worthless campaign. The young man, Mario, explained to me in the beginning that the process could take a few weeks. Yet in still, the waiting game was nearly unbearable. Mario told me he would have to alter my website's content for keyword optimization, and build some organic back links.

Not fully grasping all the technicalities initially, that was fine with me. What was most important was seeing my search engine results improve drastically in about 10 days. As a result, my business more than doubled as people used the search engines to find firms like mine. This was a true godsend, and my conversations with Mario led me to discover another great online tactic for doing big business on a small budget.

Social Media: the Small Business Gold Mine

As I mentioned in the previous paragraph, Mario had to build organic back links to my website. This was partially done by starting an account for my business on virtually every social media website out there. This was a daunting task because I'm not the most technically savvy person in the world. However, starting the campaign did increase my business to the point where I had to hire a few people to help out around the office.

Though there are over a dozen social media sites with an account for my business, Facebook is by far my favorite. I was even able to download an app called Iframes which allowed me to change my Facebook page's HTML until it looked just like my websites landing page.

This service allows the business owner to even advertise to their specific target audience. For my own business, I set a daily budget, and the website charges my account as little or as much as I determine.

Going Global

The key principal is to recognize that a larger business is not necessarily your competition. Ask yourself how you are different? If the competition is larger they will have a lot of advantages that you won't because of their scale, and size. So don't compete on those levels.

Recognize that you have a lot of potential to be better, and stronger in ways they can't— likely you are more nimble, and ready to make change, and adapt to trends as well as and customer requests and you can connect on a more personal level with customers. Use these differences to your advantage and compete as a different business.

CHAPTER 7
Financing Options for an Entrepreneur

*W*hen starting a business it is imperative that you obtain the proper amount of capital you need. There are a number of resources to gain a substantial amount of startup money, you just have to know where to look. Having money is not only crucial to your business but it can be crucial to your own survival as well.

There is no guarantee that once you start your business, it will be immediately successful. If you are unable to pay bills, or feel financially free enough to focus on your business the distraction will inevitably destroy everything you are working for.

When starting a small business you may find it necessary to find financial assistance. A Small Business Loan with the SBA (Small Business Administration) may be just what you are looking for. It's a wonderful program that will assist business owners with their start up even if they may have trouble qualifying for a more traditional style loan.

They have several different loan plans to choose from, and they will be very helpful in trying to figure out what your financial needs may be. Three of the major small business loans they provide at the start are the:

• Certified Development Company Loan, which provides businesses who are expanding at a decent rate the capital needed to purchase assets such as land and buildings.

• Basic 7(a) Loan Program, is great for starting or expanding a small business. A very basic loan is great for those looking for a simple option.

• Microloan Program, is great for those who aren't looking for a large amount of capital to start, the cap hovering around $50,000.

Angel Investors, can also be a small miracle to those looking to open a small business. Angel Investors are those who invest their own money into a small startup business. Often times these investors can be found among friends and family who believe in you.

Their focus falls on helping you, as well as your business succeed rather than the profit they will receive from their investment once the business is up and running. This can be a one-time allotment of money or can be ongoing, seeing a small company through a rough patch.

When it comes to presenting your business to an Angel Investor you are expected to have the following items below in order to even be considered a contender.

- A solid Business Plan with 3-5 year projections for the business with an exit strategy in place.

- A Pitch Deck which is a slideshow going over the size of the problem in the market, the solution you've created, then the market size of your consumers.

- It would be great to also have an Elevator Pitch prepared which is a 30 second pitch that sums up your business in a nutshell. There will be times that you meet investors on the go, that will not have the time to review all of your documentations in that setting but you may be able to peek their interests with your Elevator Pitch that will then lead to a further meeting down the road.

- Have a solid Valuation in place. What does this mean? A Business valuation is a process and a set of procedures used to estimate the economic value of an owner's interest in a business.

Example: I am looking for $100,000 for 25% ownership of my company. What this statement is saying is that you are giving 25% of your company to an investor who is going to invest $100,000 into your business which is being valued at $400,000 before it makes a single dollar as a start-up company to an investor.
25% is 1/4 of the company, so 100k is 1/4 of the valuation. It follows that 100% of the company (25 x 4) would be 400k (100 x 4).

Daymond John of Shark Tank a world renowned investor said it best when he said, "The biggest mistake is that entrepreneurs attempt to charge an investor for what they have put into their business. An entrepreneur must pitch a potential investor for what the company is worth as well as sell the dream on how much of a profit can be made.

Entrepreneurs need to try, and have something associated with their business or product trademarked or patented. This shows potential investors that you are diligent, and patient. The way that your business or product is presented is usually a sign of how you will operate. Target an investor that will reap the value of your product or business. It's an easier sale. Try to have something trademarked, or patented.

It shows you've been diligent enough, and patient. Surround yourself with a strong team ready to advise, and help you produce real results. Make the investor feel like they are buying a team. Target a investor that you, and your product adds value to their organization. Sell yourself as the ultimate product.

Crowdfunding is another option open to entrepreneurs when looking to start up a small business. Crowdfunding is a concept where a network of individuals comes together to obtain funding for a business, or campaign they are looking to support. Often times, this rally or funding is done online, and is programmed to raise money for the cause of their choosing. Another form of Crowdfunding is by giving small amounts of equity to many investors.

While expanding the number of investors, you are able to get knowledgeable opinions on your product from people who are passionate enough to invest their time, and money into making sure your business succeeds. This is becoming a more popular option among business owners. With online platforms working to assist business owners and investors to come together.

Traditional Bank Loans in previous years have never been a rational option for small-business owners. Banks couldn't be bothered by the small businesses, which opened up the market to other companies to jump in and provide the much needed small business loans.

However, as soon as the small business became a popular industry to loan to banks were quick to jump on board. Even though they have joined the race, they are not at the top of the competition. Like any other lending enterprise, it is important to establish how much your company needs for a successful startup. When you have your numbers outlined, you will appear more organized.

When asking friends or family to help by contributing financially to help you start up your business, it is important to establish clear boundaries between business and pleasure. Reaching out to your closest circle may benefit you financially, however, when people are comfortable with you they will feel more inclined to give their opinion as to how the money they are investing should be spent.

It is important to remember that just because people may believe in you, and your product, it does not mean they are inclined to contribute financially to your business. Their choice not to support you in that way is not personal. It may just be a personal preference to not involve their social circle with their business choices, or they may not have the financial freedom at that time.

When a previous client Mike Harris started his small bakery with his wife, they never thought that a small business loan would get them so far. Allowing them to grow their business, and providing them the finances to open a new bakery after their lease was up, they were able to generate over a million dollars in sales in. Their products are carried in Wal-Mart stores, and they are now able to travel and promote their baked goods.

When looking to start, or expand your small business it is important to obtain the proper funding.

By approaching any of the outlets I have mentioned, is a good way to go about obtaining it. Make sure to have all of your numbers, and approach it in an organized and professional manor.

Make sure to budget out for incidentals and make sure you will be able to stay afloat and keep your focus on your start up. Now is the time to enjoy the plethora of funding options and outlets available to the modern entrepreneur.

CHAPTER *8*
The Importance of Having a Mentor

*W*hen I think of an entrepreneur I think of many largely successful and often wealthy people who were able to gain that success by thinking somewhat outside of the box. People like, Bill Gates and Mark Zuckerberg who identified what they were passionate about, and found a way to make that it the focus of their life's pursuits.

Now without a mentor, the individual's ideas are often more free-flowing and unique, not boxed in by the constraints of "That's not what I was shown". However, not everyone has innate ideas just bursting from within them, or if they do, they may not have the confidence to pursue them. In many ways, these "celebrities", and their successes seem a bit out of reach for the general public.

For the majority of successful "normal" people there was someone in their lives that made a difference, and motivated them to then make certain life changing decisions. I would say that often it is just a matter of having that one person who believes in you, and has the ability to show you what you are truly capable of.

An additional benefit of a mentor in your career is that this person has already been there, and can hopefully guide you so that you can avoid many of the pitfalls they fell victim to. This mentor gives you someone to look to, and perhaps emulate in many of the decisions you make in the formation of your career.

Aside from this structural aid, there's also the advantage of having someone who can provide emotional, and psychological support as you develop as a new entrepreneur. The mentor will be able to understand the internal process you're going through as your business changes, and grows in a way that many others in your life may not be able to. You can avoid that awful feeling of being, "all alone at the top".

Also, if this person works within your business world, he may be able to offer tips, or open up opportunities that otherwise you would not have had access to. Within many worlds of work, that mentor can be a crucial part of your network and the ease of which you obtain your career goals.

Many successful mentor-mentee pairs began with the simple act of caring for another. World renowned poet Maya Angelou credits an elementary school teacher as being the catalyst for her love of poetry. Ray Charles mentored a young Quincy Jones with his passion for music.

Most of us know of the legend Michael Jordan, who has been considered the best basketball player on the face of this earth. What most people don't realize is that Michael could not win a title for several years, because he had the mindset that he had to do everything himself to get the win, rather than depending on his teammates.

It wasn't until Phil Jackson was hired as the head coach of the Chicago Bulls that Michael began to think outside the box. Phil came from a different upbringing, and had different philosophies on life as well as what winning truly meant.

Having the ability to use different strategies he learned along the way that no other coach had even considered, Phil implemented how Native Americans always hunted as a clan, and also began using the meditation practices he learned from great monks. He later passed those onto the players.

As a result, the team began to gel in a way no other coach could have done previously, which in turn created a family bond between the players that was up until that point, non-existent. With a new spiritual bond in place, and a deep understanding of what winning truly meant, the Bulls were able to win 6 championship titles over a 9 year period.

I had a very similar experience within my career. I always knew I wanted to be very successful, I just didn't know HOW. I knew that I could have picked up a self-help book on how to be successful, but I was a different type of learner----- I needed someone to physically show me how to do it.

It wasn't until I met the CEO of the Real Estate firm I worked at, that I knew I met the mentor I needed to mirror, in order to become what I'd been dreaming of. He lived in a gated community in the Hills with breathtaking views, and owned some of the rarest exotic cars such as a Lamborghini, Carrera GT, Ferrari, Bentley, and Rolls Royce.

On top of that, he was happily married with two children. While working at the firm I consistently sought out advice on what I could do to be better with clients, and how I could someday achieve the success he had.

He always told me to put the client first, and make sure to work longer than the next man. He always had a saying that it's the first person at the office, and the last one to leave that achieves what they want in life. Adopting his principle, I made it a way of life to work long hours, and do what others were afraid to do in order to live the, type of life I wanted.

Over the past few years of working at the firm, he saw that I had applied everything he taught me and my career was thriving. One day as he was walking down the stairs to grab his daily smoke break, he stopped by my office and asked if I wanted to join him. I put the file I was working on to the side, and walked downstairs with him.

As we walked, we also talked about the deals we both were working on and what the family plans were for the weekend. When we got downstairs, he told me that it was, "that time". I replied with, "what do you mean? What time is it?".

He said, "it's that time for you to go to the next level". He stated that he had been watching my performance on how I was able to successfully build the team he wanted me to build. We had a deep conversation about how he wouldn't be willing to pass the company down to his daughters, because none of them had any interest in the Real Estate industry. Talking to me as if I was his son, He then said to pick a car---- as a matter of fact, any car from his collection. The very collection that I so admired!

Stunned, and in a state of disbelief, it took a long moment for me to accept that he was talking to me! His car collection was worth over 4 million dollars, and here he was offering me keys to ANY car. The only stipulation was that I cover the car payments associated with the car I'd choose. So, being the young kid that I was, I immediately asked what the payment was on the Lamborghini (I'm sure you're not surprised!). He says, "the Lamborghini payment is $4,700 a month". That was MUCH too steep for me.

Next, I passed the Ferrari----with a payment that would be $2,900. I almost bit on the Ferrari, but I knew that was also out of my budget. Finally, I arrived at the car that would be mine: the Mercedes SL55 AMG. While the payment was, $1,876 a month, he agreed to make me a deal. I'd *only* have to pay $1,500 of that monthly car payment, with him covering the difference.

Now, here I was, 20 years old driving a 100 thousand dollar car, making between 15-20K a month, and living in a great community when just a few years prior I couldn't even rub two nickels together. This experience speaks to the power of having someone to learn from, mirror, and the true importance of a mentor.

Without the proper mentor in place, it is very difficult to see where you are going and how you are going to get there when pursuing any dream. Yes, it is very possible to be an entrepreneur and develop a career without a mentor... When we weigh in the many benefits of having a mentor, it doesn't seem like the wisest decision to miss out on this great asset.

CHAPTER *9*
Keep Learning and Stay on Top of Industry Trends

Our world is changing every day –
especially in business, and technology. To
compete in the long run, you have to stay up-
to-date on what is new. If you are running
your business on outdated practices,
thoughts or technology, you WILL get left
behind.

The key to a successful business is to remain
cutting edge. Again, this is where innovation
comes into play. Take the time to attend

conferences, or classes relating to your industry. If those are too costly, or you don't have the time, consider learning the information online. There are so many resources on the internet, that there is absolutely no excuse for not knowing the latest information, and trends in your industry.

The beauty, and the beast of technology is what will make or break you in this constantly developing world. Success comes from change; the ability to adapt and become different. Our world, more so than before, is changing at a rapid pace.

Those who are willing to keep up, have a better chance of survival. Those who think that their methods, and tactics are better than new technology innovations, will remain in their stubborn bubble, further halting any potential growth or advancement within their business. It is to your benefit, as well as your consumer to keep an open mind.

To stay on top of the industry trends, it is important to understand that you need to engulf yourself with education. Not all education necessarily comes in the form of a degree.

Take Bill Gates for example: He chose to follow his passion to start up a computer company and forgo his education. Although it should be known that he did later pick up where he left off, and obtained a college degree.

Education can come in the form of journals, reading material, catching the news on a regular basis, constant research, Internet research, attending lectures, or surrounding yourself with those who you wish to learn from.

Education is a priceless tool, and you can gift that to yourself at any time. If you are a self-made entrepreneur, you get the ability to not only decide your education, but also the ability to decide the education of the employees you choose to hire.

It's a known fact that people who hold a college degree or higher, ultimately will reap a higher annual salary than those who do not hold. Of course, just like any statistic, this trend follows the standard deviation of the statistic. There are some outliers who will never obtain a college education, and become some of the richest men, and women on the planet. The point, is that education is, your segue to learning new ideas, approaches, and current trends---That you may not have known about otherwise.

Here is a simple depiction to allow your thoughts to develop around this concept.... The computer and Internet boom literally took off with a "boom!". Some chose to jump on the bandwagon, and chance their luck with this new development. Others thought they knew better, and decided to remain steady with their current business practices, while avoiding the "boom' at all costs.

The overall result was that those who took the chance, made it rich. On the other hand, those who didn't had two options: One, you jump on the bandwagon now and count your losses, but start to gain strength; or two, keep to your tactics and methods by avoiding the boom, and slowly kill your business.

So, how do you stay on top of these "industry" trends you may be asking yourself. It is a simple answer...believe in change, be willing to take a risk, and never stop learning about your industry. Be active, and present within your industry. In other words, make a name for yourself. Be someone your competitors need to watch out for.

Being vocal in your industry goes hand in hand with networking. NEVER take this for granted. Allow yourself to socialize with fellow business minded people like yourself, or amongst your competitors is key to staying on top of your industry. After all, you don't ever want someone to have the inside scoop before you do. Additionally, it is impossible to have too many connections.

A great path to success is to study past trends, learn about change and embrace new ideologies. This happens through reading. Reading, (I know, I know-- a very old fashioned technique) yet it has much to offer the modern day entrepreneur. Reading will exploit you to opportunities, common practices, and general information about your industry.

Don't assume you know it all, you don't and never will. However, you can embrace new knowledge, and learn from it. Reading may allow you the opportunity to be the next trend setter. Create that million dollar strategy, and then market it to others. Surrounding yourself with words and books, will also enhance your ability to spot trends. Now, that goes to say that not all trends will be beneficial. You just may develop the skill to spot a trend that may be a hit, but a tombstone tomorrow.

Staying on top of the industry trends doesn't just mean from a monetary stand point. Sometimes these changes that surround us are for the better of the environment. Maintaining the environment and preserving the resources that remain is a very big trend now. Jumping on board with this trend is a step in the right direction.

Many times the government is willing to give you a kick back, or tax break, if you prove you have taken positive actions in turning your company green. This is an attractive feature to many consumers now, and if you advertise that you are taking such efforts to maintain a green business, chances are your business will succeed farther than those who are avoiding the green trend.

Another trend that is vitally important to your business is in safety. More often than not, safety keeps transforming to develop efforts to making the everyday grind of the industry more bearable. You will have a higher success rate, greater employee satisfaction, and lower turnovers, by following the newest safety trends.

To be successful in these times, embrace changes. Don't be the only one to avoid a trend, and choose to remain stagnant. Take risks, as great risks will often lead to great opportunity. Train yourself to spot trends that will provide a long term opportunity for you and your business. But most importantly, don't fear change.

CHAPTER *10*
The Pro's & Con's to a Business Partnership

*W*hen starting a new business, several factors need to be thought through before making any legal or financial commitments. One of those factors is whether or not the company will consist of a sole proprietor ownership, or partner ownership. Both options have advantages, and disadvantages. While neither option is better than the other, entrepreneurs should consider their goals, and business needs in order to best decide which business structure to go with.

One of the first things entrepreneurs should consider is their legal liability as the owner of a company. When going into business alone, you will be solely responsible for taxes, debt, and other financial obligations of the company. Therefore, think about potential liability issues that are a risk to companies like yours. If your company is likely to take on a large amount of financial obligations, you not only will want to find legal protection against those risks, but also have a partner assisting in paying for those obligations.

As you think about liability cost, also consider startup cost, and other ongoing administration financial needs of the company. Partnerships are generally more expensive than sole proprietorship, as there are more individuals involved in the business, therefore there are more administrative, and legal tasks to keep up with.

After considering financial obligations of the company, think about the needs of the company by establishing goals, and envisioning your business in the future. The more owners a business has, the more variations of goals that business will need to live up to. Therefore, when going into business with someone, know what their goals are for the company, and work together to understand as well as support each other's goals.

These goals will assist you in understanding the flexibility of the company. For example, if both partners have strict profit goals, the company will be less flexible as they will need more dedication to meet those goals.

On the other hand, if the company has relaxed financial goals, the partners can focus their attention on other areas of the company, and have more flexibility in the direction of the company. Also, each business partner, or sole owner, should think about what they expect the company to look like in one year, five years, and ten years. The company's goals will evolve over time, but by predicting those goals both business owners will be better equipped to lead the business to success.

If you decide to take on a business partner, establish each owner as either a general partner or a limited partner. General partners are not only financially obligated to the company, but also take on management responsibilities of the company. Limited partners are merely investors, and have little say on what goes on within the company. While general partners are liable to the business' financial obligations, limited partners are not.

Before your company takes on any limited partners, have an approximate idea of how many limited partners will be investing in your company. Limited partners often require more administrative duties, and, therefore higher cost. If your company plans to take on limited partners, consider that the more limited partners you have, the less administrative costs, will be required for each one limited partner. If you do not plan to have several limited partners, you may want to only allow general partners to be involved in the company.

Once you outline your business obligations and goals, you will have a good idea of whether or not you need a business partner. If you decide your business will profit from a partner, know what qualifications your business partner should have. The obvious qualification are professional qualification, which depend upon your specific business. For example, business qualifications for a partner in a hair salon will be significantly different than qualifications for a computer based company.

Regardless of what your business is, there are a few universal qualifications that should be considered. How trustworthy is your partner? What are their communication skills? Finally, how well does that person compliment you, and your work strategy?

It is crucial that you trust, and can communicate well with your business partner. Without trust, the partner could easily take advantage of you, and the company. While you will want to find a trustworthy partner, extra protection through legally binding contracts should also be considered. How many times has someone given you their word, and didn't deliver on the promise? Make certain that everything is in writing---it protects you both.

Also, regardless of your vision and qualifications, you will not be able to anticipate every problem or always know how to best handle a situation. Therefore, choose a business partner who is different from you, but also compliments your strengths and weaknesses. Then, any gaps that you may have, will be resolved by your partner's involvement.

Neither sole proprietor nor partner businesses guarantee success, or failure. Instead, success comes from a business plan that is well thought through. Every company is unique, therefore determining your need for a partner is established through thorough investigation of your company, and what is to be expected not only when the business is launched, but many years down the line.

When running a Real Estate firm I decided to partner with the individual that initially trained me for the job. I figured that he was the perfect match for me as a business partner. After all, he had trained me, all of the new employees, and helped them meet their goals when they struggled, or fell short. Our partnership also included an exorbitant amount of overhead costs, but we were financially fine as our commissions from closings were large.

We had 17 different agents, with 17 different personalities working for us, and they all not only observed/were affected by our business decisions, but they also had their own set of opinions, grievances, and critiques. They made certain we heard each one! We were certainly generating more money as a partnership, but overtime, the expenses and continued counseling type sessions with each agent became more tedious than we expected.

I was in a partnership, but at times I definitely still felt like a mentee, rather than an equal. My employees took notice to my stress, and soon began to realize that I was doing roughly about 85% of the work, but splitting all the profits 50/50 with my business partner.

Out of concern for my wellbeing, an intervention took place. All the agents asked for an immediate meeting while my business partner was away. In the intervention session, the agents addressed their concerns with the "partnership" I had, and did not understand how I was doing all the work for them, and yet alone splitting all profits with my business partner. They gave me an ultimatum... Either I reconsider my partnership, or they walk away.

So, a decision had to be made. Would I keep my partnership, or lose my entire staff? After a moment to think it over, the decision was made.

The next day, I had the grueling conversation with my business partner that not only could the partnership no longer be active, but also that I'd be willing to buy him out to help with the process. He was devastated with my decision, and was completely blind-sided by it. However, when running a business, there are going to be decisions that have to be made, in order to keep your business functional and thriving. Had I thought this process through before making the initial decision of the partnership, I would have saved a lot of time, energy, and money in the process.

CHAPTER *11*
Saving For a Rainy Day

*A*ny and every entrepreneur knows that there are certain things to consider when going into business, especially within the first year. Many have heard the old adage that they should not plan on making money in the first year, and that still reigns true. However, many online businesses may find that not always true.

No matter how things are going on day 1 or day 1001, there are a few things to keep in mind. The only constant is change. In other words a business person can count on one thing, that one thing being that the future is unknown. Things will occur as well as inevitably change. That means that the "rainy day" syndrome is very important.

The Rainy Day

There are a few ways to look at the first several years of business, and each of them has an up and a down side. One can take every single dime that a business makes, and put it back into the business. It's like the, "Tycoon" computer game. The minute that a business sells a glass of lemonade for $1, they invest that full dollar back into getting more sugar, and lemons.

This is one way of doing business, but the down side is that if something happens, there is no way out. If an imaginary lemonade stand gets stolen overnight, then the tycoon has nothing other than a load of lemons, and sugar. This can be the end all and be all of the business itself. That rainy day is sure to come.

It is the simple odds of the matter. Each day that passes by, the odds of something going awry increases. Machines, and equipment age and need repair. Employees steal, and quit at unknown times for unknown reasons. Plans fall through. It's the nature of life, and business.

Being Prepared

A new business or even an existing business can consider a savings plan as a normal expense. Setting aside a given amount each, and every fiscal period is something that must be done. Every business, even the biggest and greatest corporations have seen downfalls. It is the ones that are prepared for these moments that come through on the other side.

One can think of companies as large as Microsoft and Wal-Mart and look back, and see that they have run into major issues in the past. The reason that they are still here and as large as they are, is due to the fact that they had the resources to survive the rainy days. That makes it possible to not just survive, but to thrive through these times when expenses are higher, and the revenue is lower.

A good company should consider how they will survive if they have no sales or revenue of any kind for 30 days. Think about this like a game show. The key to winning is to survive for just 30 days with nothing coming in. If you make it through the 30 days then you win the big cash prize.

Now What?

It is simple. Choose a period of time. It can be a week, or a month, or biweekly. Set an amount, and make sure that the amount is something that the business can handle. Each and every time period, put that amount of money away for the rainy day.

The key to this is to never, I repeat NEVER compromise this schedule. If something occurs, then the money is there, but never "skip a week", or "short" this week's savings. If you allow this to happen one time, then it becomes an easy compromise, and a vicious cycle that results in the weekly savings never being done.

Remember; never take money from the savings unless it is a dire emergency. This is the hardest part. Everything becomes an emergency, and the next thing that the business knows, the savings is gone. These are the same things that happen to a single person or family when they dip into their savings.

Which leads me to touch upon corporations, and board members. Even if the business is not a full corporation, it can have a "board." These can be people that are trusted, and that have a good sense of business. In the event that something occurs, they can vote on whether or not the event warrants dipping into the savings.

Choose your trusted friends carefully. It is sure that a group of drinking buddies will approve a withdrawal from the savings for a trip to Reno rather than friends who understand your path, and want to see you succeed.

In the End

In the end, it is the welfare of the future that is being protected by having a business nest egg. It is not the events that we foresee that we plan for, it is the events that we never see coming that we have to plan for. One day, everything is great and the next day, everything falls apart. If you wish to succeed and have longevity, then having funds set aside behooves you.

This is the difference between the businesses that you have never heard of, and the ones that you currently shop at. They all planned carefully and acted carefully. They all have a fund that is there is case something happens, and they've all utilized it.

CHAPTER *12*
Welcome To the World of The 1099

*T*he world of the IRS Form 1099 is an important one and should not be overlooked. You can encumber serious fines if you neglect this Form that will impact you as an entrepreneur. The form in its most common use is the Form 1099-MISC and can be downloaded at irs.gov. The guide included will be of great assistance but I'll expand on this for you to make it easier to understand.

The MISC in the form covers a lot. The IRS provides instructions that are very specific. When the IRS makes a rule or provides detailed examples, it is there for your information, and protection. No matter what size business you have, small or large, you are required to submit a 1099 MISC to everyone you paid in the previous calendar year, over $600.00, that is not a defined employee.

A defined employee is one who receives a W-2, and you both pay taxes on that income. A 1099 employee is someone you hired for 'casual labor' or a particular service where you engaged them to work for your company.

Attention to detail in these types of issues can have a profound outcome that would be a detriment to your company if not followed. The IRS has the power, and latitude to place liens on your company. The Form 1099 also plays into the considerable scope of the Information Reporting Program of the Bureau of Internal Revenue. You are a defined business or Corporation, S Corp, therefore expected to track income. A good slogan to keep in your mind: *"Taxpayer expense equals income to another. Income has to be reported."*

Presuming you are established, the use of your Taxpayer Identification Number or TIN will be a required part of your submission on Form 1099. If you don't have a TIN, you better get one! (Form W-9).

Another reason why the Form 1099 MISC is an integral part of Reporting Program is that there is approximate $450 billion tax "gap." (Taxes paid versus taxes owed.) Small Business has been very resistant to do this, which only lends itself for future issues with and those are not worth it.

Get out your Day-Timer or make a note on your smartphone that anyone who you have paid money to in the previous tax year in the amount of $600.00 or greater is required to receive a 1099 MISC postmarked no later than Jan. 31 of each year. Stay organized. Your business accounting software or your accountant will keep track of this but ultimately, you're responsible as the owner. It is a good idea to really spend the time and become familiar with the many assets of the Form 1099 MISC. Go here and check it out: http://www.irs.gov/form1099misc.

If you are a nonprofit, you are still required to report a 1099-MISC to anyone you paid during the course of the previous tax year. Just because you are a non-profit, 501-C or D does not leave you off the hook. Make your yearend easy. You may be an owner who has a busy life with a family, kids, business, student, or the like. It does not matter.

Do not allow your personal responsibilities to stand in the way of this important business transaction. Organization will help you with the good habits of a responsible business owner. The beauty of being an entrepreneur is that you are in charge of your own destiny. Taking time to follow these vital steps throughout the year will make your tax filing, and reporting responsibility flow all the more seamlessly.

Here are a few quick tips:

1. When you engage in services with an individual, have them give you the necessary information at the beginning of the transaction, so you can issue the Form 1099 MISC without having to go back to them. Make sure you collect their name, address, city, state, and zip and make a copy of their Social Security card.

2. If you manage these tasks, or have one staff person handling it, make sure you have imputed all the information onto your accounting software.

3. Be diligent. Keep records!

4. If you don't have the self-discipline to do this, then hire a firm that will handle your tax reporting. If you cannot be bothered, paying an accountant is always an option, and you can write off the expense! Hey! Why not support other businesses?

Electronic Filing for 1099:

The electronic age has made this so much easier and it is a plus for the business owner. With each form there is a booklet of instructions for you to wade through. But they also offer services as E-File, which reduces the amount of paperwork on your end. Filing Information Returns Electronically (FIRE) is exclusive to many forms including the 1099. Take advantage of the service the IRS provides. They can walk you through it, and it is more efficient. Always keep a copy of what you submit along with the receipt that you filed, and jot down date and time in case something goes wrong.

More information about E-Services can be found here.
 http://www.irs.gov/Government-Entities/Indian-Tribal-Governments/-Electronic-Filing-and-E-Services.

Record keeping! The main purpose of maintaining highly organized records is not only because it makes sense and is good business, but will help provide any needed answers in the future as well preparing a response if you are audited by the IRS. Associated documents you used to issue your Form 1099-MISC such as canceled checks, records of direct deposits, invoices, or statements should be kept in a secure filing cabinet.

In short, the IRS Form 1099 is important. You MUST issue the form each year to those people who were paid more than $600.00, or suffer the consequences that might occur that can bring serious trouble to your business. And again, if you have no interest in doing it properly, pay someone who does. It is worth the money.

While living in San Jose, CA and having an amazing career in Real Estate during its booming time of the late 90's, I was not properly educated with the importance of staying on top of spending and keeping a report of everything. I did not have an accountant and let's just say, I was young and unwise. As discussed in previous chapters, making between 15-20K a month and being paid completely as an independent contractor, I wasn't at all smart about my money.

I thought I'd just deal with it when I was ready to. A few years went by, and as the Real Estate market began to tank in 2008, I was not making the same amount of money I was accustomed to making. Needless to say, the IRS never forgot about the amount of money I made over the years, and the large past due statement came in the mail when I least expected it.

My rainy day had come. I was in the middle of short selling my home, returning my Mercedes back to the dealership because I could no longer afford it, and interviewing for other jobs just to stay afloat. I'm sure you're probably wondering how much I owed over the years? Here's a hint--- that notice was in the amount that most dentists make in a year. It was *that* bad.

With interest and fee's all included, I was not in a position to negotiate so I took a deal to pay it back over a spread out, agreed upon time. If I would've stayed on top of my books I wouldn't have needed to pay major penalties, and fines. More money would've been saved had I just been diligent. It certainly was an expensive lesson for me, but one I'm grateful I learned-----I am now able to share it with you.

The IRS doesn't, "forget" about money made, or owed. Keep an honest record of all your transactions, at all times. You've got dreams to fulfill! Keep it simple!

CHAPTER *13*
When to Throw In the Towel

*N*ow that you've identified, and understood
the importance of the IRS form 1099, it is now
time to understand when to throw in the
towel. When we've identified our whys, and
purposes,   changed our mind, and ultimately
changed our lives, agreed to not allow fears
to stop us from excelling, have put in hard
work, but for some reason, things are not
moving as they should, it is that time to
decide if you should continue on.

Every seasoned entrepreneur has a failed
venture that they'd be able to share with you,

as well as the lessons they learned from that experience. I speak from personal experience when I tell you that it is a daunting task, and even cuts like a butcher knife to say you've failed.

This is why I encourage you to switch your language, and to begin to identify this as a, "learning experience". You haven't truly, "failed" if you tried. With entrepreneurship, if you've never had an experience where a venture didn't work out, you will truly never appreciate what success feels like. It's a very humbling experience, and builds the type of character that will only make you that much better with your next venture.

There are a couple questions that you'll need to ask yourself, and again honestly answer:

1. Has your business generated a single dollar in revenue in the first 120 days of being operated? If not, that would be the best time to reevaluate your business model, as well as the type of clients you are looking to attract.

I have always believed that a person should follow their passion in life whether it is in personal relationships and /or life choices such as going into business for yourself. It takes a lot of courage, and passion to take the leap into the entrepreneurial whirlpool that drowns most first time businesses. However, when your passion, and purpose do not have the proper processing behind them, you're ultimately doing more harm than good.

2. How long has it been since you took an honest look at why your business is failing? When we are emotionally connected to our dream, we may not even be aware that there is a problem. We aimlessly plant seeds, but on infertile ground thus never seeing a harvest. That, "dream" becomes detrimental, and the time to wake up and face reality is there.

The figures don't lie. Smallbiztrends.com states that in 2013 alone 40 percent of startup businesses failed, and out of that 60 percent that survived the first year, 95 percent of them are destined to fail within the VERY next year!

The sad news is that when these small businesses go under, they have also taken down with them the resources, assets, and passion of the entrepreneurial spirit that drives the American Dream. There is a fine line walking the tight rope between following your passion in business, and being fiscally responsible. You need to be an impassioned observer of the business on a regular basis so that you can truly evaluate, and reevaluate the "REAL" success, and failure of the business.

It is not a failure to throw in the towel on something that is not working. If you continue to throw money into the exact same plans, advertising, clients, employees and you're STILL not bringing in revenue, then it is time to take a hard look at the business.

Do not get caught up in the following of your passions on such an emotional level, that you lose your head, and are blinded to these very real issues.

The good news is, that perhaps it isn't time "to throw in the towel", but rather time to readjust, shake things up, re-invent.

If you're fearful of learning experiences, or in other words failure, you become clouded by your emotions making it difficult to see the truth of your particular "cliff" that you just might be running straight for.

My advice is based on MUCH research, as well as a couple past "failed" businesses. You'll be able to save time, money, and energy if you apply the following steps I've included:

- Always keep a good objective eye on the startup by scheduling quarterly assessment periods. It is like a maintenance tune-up on your car. Most people take the time to schedule routine maintenance checks for their automobiles because they have a big investment in the vehicle.

- It is the exact same philosophy when scheduling a quarterly assessment of your business. Is it losing money, or making money? Is your advertising working for you, or against you? Do you have a way of tracking that said advertising to see if it is working, or not? Are you targeting the right audience, demographics? Are you buying the right products at the right price? Are you comparable in quality, and price as those of your competitors? Do you stand out? Why? Why Not? Are your employees rising to the occasion, or are they dead weight? These are all questions you want to consider on a quarterly time frame.

Business ownership was never promised to be easy, and if it was, they lied. You're going to have to put in the work, to get the best results you DESERVE. Take time to schedule your success. This is going to mean that every 120 days or so, you've opened up your schedule to clearly look at your business without the emotion, but rather as if you were an outsider or a potential customer.

- Are you making money? Can it survive under the circumstances it's under at the time of assessment? Can processes evolve, or change? What IS working? What is NOT working? What has NEVER worked?

These are hard questions to ask yourself when it is like your "baby." Near, and dear to your heart, and what you feel so passionately about. Here is the truth: If your "baby" is not growing, and thriving after a good hard look, then you might want to understand that being done with something that is not working is not failing. It is foresight. It is growth.

If you truly take what you've learned from the assessment, and apply it wisely to your next endeavor then you have certainly not failed at all, but rather you succeeded in knowledge, wisdom. You've also opened up more time to focus on finding a venture that WILL work for you.

Johnny Cash is known as one of the most legendary country music singers and songwriters of ALL time, but yet his life was riddled with ups, and downs including time spent in prison, life threatening circumstances, addictions, and illnesses. Through all of his failures he gleaned treasures, and turned them into hit after hit with songs that touched people. Through his failures he became a success.

Donald Trump has filed bankruptcy 4 times and is still one of the most successful entrepreneurs in modern American History. Understand this: The American Dream is layered like an onion with nightmares of financial ruin, but the idea of the American Dream is still alive and well.

Some of our most successful artists, leaders, influencers, and entrepreneurs have met failure or-----a learning experience. You have to know what is working and what is not working before you can truly call anything a success or a failure.

How long has it been since you set aside a couple of days to do a real assessment of your entrepreneurial endeavors? Be as objective as you possibly can. If you can't be impartial about the shortcomings, and strengths of where your business really is then by all means find an expert that can give you help in an impartial point of view. Do not be afraid of the outcome, even if it means it is time to throw in the towel.

How I Learned the Hard Way:

After a failing real estate market in 2008 and losing everything I'd ever worked for, I was hungry for success again. I made the choice to move back to Columbus, OH only to live with my mother, and honestly it was one of the most humbling experiences for me. As you all may remember, I arrived in San Jose, California with just a backpack, and goals. Having to back track wasn't easy, but it was so needed for me.

During my stay, I realized how much I needed to grow. I had fears to face. Priorities to set straight. I needed to heal, recoup, and grow on a spiritual as well as intellectual level if I wanted to not only reach success, but keep success.

While doing inner work, I also developed a plan of action to start over again. I was drawn to investment firms after diving deep into research on the industry. I researched all different types of investment firms, as well as the strategies they used to make a profit for the company all the while keeping their clients happy.

I knew this was the path for me. After connecting with a local firm, I quickly noticed the amount they'd get paid with nice hefty bonus checks attached to them. After continued research, I discovered there was also a unique form of investing that was a little off the grid, but provided a larger return than most. It also doubled the amount of money a typical agent could make.

Naturally, I was eager to learn more about this particular form of investing. It was catered to the clients that were required to generate over 50M in their portfolios just to be considered. The form of investing was particularly liquidating assets only to trade them on a 40 week fixed based investment.

In other words, clients would get a monthly return on their investment, but they would need to have their money tied up in this particular investment for the full term of the 40 weeks.

Doing my research I realize that high level executives, politicians, and attorneys are all involved with this form of investing.

Not really having any type of clientele to support the requirements, I began connecting with groups, and brokers that could provide more information on these particular deals, and investments. Coming to the conclusion that all of these particular transactions happened overseas I knew I was dead in the water.

It wasn't until I connected with a firm out of Los Angeles that I knew I may have a shot. Excited about the possibilities, and wanting to reach success again, I emotionally headed back to Los Angeles with nothing more than $650 in my pocket, and my, "house". In other words, my car. My thought was, if I could do it once, I'm sure I could do it again.

When I arrived in LA, the majority of the money I had went into the gas tank just to get there. I also had nowhere to sleep, except for the back seat of the car I came in. After 7 months of being at the firm, and surviving on a menu of peanut butter and tuna, I was once again broke, and working another 100% commission based position.

I washed up at local gyms on a 7-day free pass, slept under my desk at the firm, leaving before the employees came in, and re-entering once the offices opened. On the weekends, it was back to sleeping in my car. I did all I could do to survive, and I couldn't believe that I ended up in this space again. I did NOT want to throw in the towel. I'd come back to succeed, but unfortunately, was suffering.

It wasn't until one night as I was sitting at a red light that it hit me. Literally. A drunk driver crashed right into me, and totaled the automobile I was in. What she didn't realize was that not only did she total my car, but she also totaled my home. Now with no car to sleep in, no money, no real food, I watched my car get towed off to the wrecking yard, and THAT is when I reached my breaking point.

As fate would have it, I saw a homeless man roll out of his blanket on the sidewalk near the accident, and I realized I was no different. It was time to throw in the towel. I canceled out my ego, chalked it up as a learning experience, and headed back to Ohio on a one-way trip ticket via Greyhound---paid for by my mother.

The entire trip back, I completely re-evaluated my idea of what it meant to be successful. It had little to do with money. Albert Einstein said it best: "Try not to become a man of success, but rather a man of value". I adopted that mantra, and changed my life.

CHAPTER *14*
Be Your Own Cheerleader and Success Will Come to You

*H*ere is the truth: If you don't do it, nobody else will. You have to stand up for yourself, your product, and your business as a whole. You are the only one who can truly sell it to others – clients, potential employees, and possible investors. As an entrepreneur, you must stay positive about your business and yourself. You are the ultimate decision behind success, and failure and you must believe you have success in yourself.

It's All About Believing in Yourself, Your Product and Your Business

Think about it this way: Do you know of anyone who tried to learn how to drive a car, and didn't succeed? Personally, I don't know of any person who started learning how to drive a vehicle, and couldn't drive in the end. In fact, I have not even heard of any person that failed to learn how to drive a car. I can venture to say that you probably haven't either.

So, the question becomes...... Why does everyone succeed in learning how to drive, but never fails at it?

The answer is very simple. Everybody who is learning the skills and techniques involved in driving a car eventually succeeds because he/she is absolutely sure – I REPEAT absolutely sure – that he/she will be able to drive long before he/she got behind the wheel.

Before you even thought about learning how to drive, you saw everyone around you driving. Even though driving is complicated, you were convinced that it'd be easy, and you'd succeed in learning it without any difficulty. From the outset, you were confident in your ability to succeed in learning how to drive, and you were successful in the process.

Let's go deeper. Why is everyone successful in learning the complicated skills involved in driving, and only few people successful in business?

The answer lies in the power of believing in yourself. Before you kick-started the process of learning how to drive, you fully believed – without any shadow of a doubt – that you would succeed. Thus, there was no room for failure when you set out to learn the intricate skills of driving a vehicle.

On the other hand, the case is different when a lot of people venture into a business. Their mind is flooded with doubts. They truly don't believe in their own skills, and abilities to make the business a success. Finally, they don't believe their product will be a commercial success.

The problem with this thinking is that we absolutely cannot expect others to believe in our business, and products if we don't even believe in them ourselves.

We are a world of people that easily tears ourselves, and others down. Failures are remembered way more than accomplishments. Example: Most people know of former Representative Anthony Weiner for the sex scandals he was involved in, but not how he got to be a member of our U.S. Congress or what he voted for or against while there.

Believe in Yourself and Others Will Be Forced to Believe in You

Let us go back to the analogy between learning how to drive a vehicle and succeeding in whatever endeavors you choose to pursue in life. From the very beginning, you were sure of success even before you sat in the driver's seat. And what was the end result? Success!

Use this same mindset when you are starting up a business venture. No matter the obstacles you encounter along the way, you should maintain a strong personal belief system within yourself, as well as a unshakeable confidence that you will be successful. Once others start to see your positive energy and that confidence in yourself, your ideas, and your products, they will be begin to believe in you. Strongly believing in your own capabilities will convince other people to believe in you as well.

Scientific Research Throws More Light on Why Some People Fail and Others Succeed

A recent survey conducted by IBM shows that the biggest barriers to success is poor mindset and attitudes. Of the more than 1500 management executives that were interviewed in this survey, 58 percent believe that the success or failure of projects depend on the mindset, and attitudes of the individuals executing the project. They confirmed that a project is more likely to fail if the person, or group of persons involved in the project have doubts in the success of the project.

Another survey published in by Dr Dobbs Journal also confirms that the success of any project lies, in the attitude and mindset of the people carrying out the project. In this survey, 70 percent of the respondents claim that they have participated in projects they believe would fail right from the start. When asked the outcome of such projects, these respondents said nearly all of such projects ended in failure.

These surveys also agree with the fact that your own belief in your skills, abilities and your product determine the success of any business venture you embark on.

Case Studies: People Who Achieve Great Success by Believing in Themselves and Their Business

Harland David Sanders: Do you know that Harland David Sanders – popularly known as Colonel Sanders of Kentucky Fried Chicken's fame – chicken recipe was rejected 1009 times? I bet the question running through your mind right now is why the heck did he continue after such huge number of rejections? The answer is simple: He believed in himself and his product. He had a why. He had process. He scheduled his success. Canceled out his fears.

Finally his perseverance paid off with massive commercial success of his chicken recipe.

Bill Gates: Have you ever heard of the company Traf-O-Data? I'm guessing your answer is no, as most people haven't. "TOD" was the first company founded by Bill Gates. Of course you should know why you didn't hear about Traf-O-Data: It was his learning experience, however the failure of Traf-O-Data didn't stop Bill Gates from believing in himself and his idea.

With perseverance, hard work and unwavering belief in himself, he was able to create one of the most successful tech companies, becoming the richest man in the world in the process.

Henry Ford: Well, Henry Ford also has his own share of learning experiences. He failed in his early business ventures and subsequently fell into poverty. His belief in himself and his ideas pushed him on the right track, and later he established the Ford Motor Company, one of the biggest producers of American-made cars.

Do you see the trend here? These individuals had an unwavering belief, and confidence in themselves and their ideas – despite experiencing numerous setbacks at the beginning. This all led them to the path of greatness. Now, it's your turn. Your own belief, and ideas can also lead you to the greatness you desire. The key is to not just say that you do, but truly inhabiting belief behind your passion.

CHAPTER *15*
Learn To Walk in Faith

*T*aking a chance in your life, and deciding to become an entrepreneur is a big step. It's one that really should be done alongside a strong level of faith. The fact of the matter is, being an entrepreneur can be riddled with struggle and hardship. Trust that faith is going to get you through those difficult times, and will help you come out on the other side successful.

I, myself, know this all too well. I was raised a Christian and put a lot of time and effort into my faith. When the time came that I decided to be an entrepreneur and start my own business, I had no idea just how important my faith would be in this undertaking.

It's a story I have heard time and time again – people wanting to make a new start in their lives, but scared of the journey. Those who start that new journey with a strong faith in God, find their way through the difficult times, and end up happy and with a better life for themselves as well as their family.

Turns out, tough times can affect the best of us, and my endeavors were no different. There were times where it certainly would have been much easier to give up, but I made a decision to just walk by faith. I felt God had led me to start this business, and He was going to help me succeed in it. Thanks to that faithfulness, things got better, the business was successful, my faith increased, and my relationship with God grew stronger.

A close friend of mine, "Sierra", was faced with having to become an entrepreneur; it wasn't something she had really voluntarily went looking for. She is the wife of a Navy seaman and got pregnant with twins. Unfortunately, one of those precious babies died soon after birth. The other twin stopped talking as he got older, and was diagnosed with Autism.

Sierra was now in a situation where her husband was gone more than he was home, all the while mothering a child that needed her constant attention. The situation didn't allow for her to work outside the home, but due to medical bills, they couldn't survive on her husband's salary alone.

Sierra took a step out on faith, and made the decision to start her own business. She had no idea what to expect, but she felt God had presented her with an opportunity and she seized it. Today, she isn't financially wealthy, but her family lives comfortably. The bills are paid, her son is progressing well, and she is happy. Her business is successful, and she credits God for it all, as she followed His calling for her.

I would also like to introduce you to Tom. He had jumped from job to job throughout his life, and finally found his passion for videography. Tom worked a full-time job as a videographer for years for a company, but he wasn't happy. About two and a half years ago he decided to join his wife in her search for a church.

He had thrown away God, and religion some time ago, but with one visit to this church he found himself wanting to reconnect. A few months later, Tom was baptized and was quickly rebuilding a relationship with God.

About six months later, Tom had an opportunity. He had received a sum of money from a land sale. At this time, his family lived paycheck to paycheck. They barely got by financially, but they were happy. With the new financial door opened, he took the money, and started his own business.

He felt God was giving him a chance to pursue his dreams, so he spent the money to purchase his own video equipment and decided to make a go at it. He got a couple of jobs, but nothing regular. Frustration set in as bills started piling up, with not enough money to pay them.

He started to question his decision, but time and time again he and his wife went back to the faith in knowing that God would provide – as He always did. Somehow, someway there was always just enough money for groceries, and when something came up, the money seemed to appear as well. As time went on, Tom was able to make a successful business of his videography services.

Find your faith, and keep your faith!

Most people would be too scared to go against the status quo, and step out on faith. The fear of having no money or not succeeding keeps them from pursuing their dreams, and even their purpose. They tend to ignore or not understand the true power of living a life of faith.

If you put your trust in God, you won't be let down. He will be there with you through the life changes and through the difficulties of being an entrepreneur. He will help you succeed – or if He has another plan for you, He will walk with you to get you there as well.

If I, Sierra, or Tom had not walked by faith, we would never have known the success we eventually would achieve. We could still be struggling, dreaming of something different, but never knowing if it could be reality. None of us knew how we were going to make ends meet or make our endeavors successful, but God did. He knew when pointing us in these directions that our needs would be met and our dreams achieved.

Whatever your religious preferences might be (if any), the fact of the matter is faith works! I in no way shape or form am trying to conform anyone, nor convince anyone to convert to Christianity. However, in order to stay consistent with this book, I have to stay authentic me. That said? I will share ALL that has worked for me, and is continuing to work. Again, faith works.

CHAPTER *16*
What is Your Legacy Going to Be?

*L*egacy. That one word is a profound, bold and an admirable word. To live a legacy, to become a legacy, and to leave a legacy. All is to be attained, and obtained through those strong-willed enough to take that chance, to take that risk, to walk that less traveled path. But who can achieve such a word? What, exactly is meant by the word "legacy"?

A legacy is an ideology, a sense of accomplishment, something that can be passed on from one generation to the next. It is something that can be retold, something that can be looked up to, and something that individuals can strive to be a part of. It can also be flipped to mean something to live for, something to strive toward, and something to learn from. That one word is something many individuals, entrepreneurs, CEO's, and world leaders just hope to leave behind them.

Many people in the world are often forgotten after they are no longer with us. Of course, their family, and dear friends will still carry a torch for their name, as well as cherish memorable experiences with them. However sadly, most people will soon be forgotten. Their personal legacy will carry on, but only to those that the individual personally impacted; which is usually as previously mentioned, family and dear friends.

Coming from a business perspective, it is SO important to be mindful of this as an entrepreneur. If you are an entrepreneur, looking to make a name for yourself, striving to achieve the unattainable, and pass your business practices and ethics down to your predecessors, leaving a legacy should be of utmost importance.

Think of Steve Jobs. Many of us have never had the privilege to actually meet the genius behind Apple, however, most of us could give you a sentence or two describing the man. He left behind a strong, powerful legacy. He took a garage computer company, and monopolized the world with a single word, "Apple".

It could be stated with complete confidence that Steve Jobs was one of the greatest entrepreneurs of our time. Innovator, driver, inventor, marketer, adviser and genius are just a few words that can truly describe him. He was a business man who made his dreams become a reality. His legacy? Apple.

Apple was a company that introduced the computer "Macintosh" in the 1980s. Through many learning experiences, and success, Steve Jobs remained the man responsible to drive Macintosh to the multi-billion dollar industry that it is today.

It is completely possible to start leaving your legacy now. The impression you make on others is part of your legacy. How you've upgraded their lives. Inspired them. Made their lives better because of the experience with you. In relation to your company, the same outlook can be applied. How did your business upgrade your consumer's experience?

Quickly, let's go back to Bill Gates, another entrepreneur, who is still leaving his legacy with us. Although not deceased like Steve Jobs, Bill Gates portrays a different type of legacy. Jobs left a legacy mainly of success, and accomplishment for a company, Apple. Bill Gates leaves an entirely different legacy. Yes, he is certainly one of one of the world's most refined, and sought after business entrepreneurs, but he also leaves us with a philanthropic legacy as well.

Alongside of making billions of dollars single handedly, crafting his Microsoft industry with a heart of gold, and being a generous donor. Bill Gates leaves a legacy to demonstrate that with **making** billions, you can also take that wealth, and **help** billions. Bill Gates is one of the most notable philanthropists. He and his wife, Melinda, have started a research foundation (The Bill and Melinda Gates Foundation) that impacts many universities, like "Caltech" which helps sponsor and fund scientific research.

It is not fair to truly compare Steve Jobs and Bill Gates; however, for the sake of speaking about legacy, it is important to note the true difference. Steve Jobs left behind a financial and successful legacy. Bill Gates is leaving behind a successful and philanthropic legacy.

Bill Gates is fulfilling not only his entrepreneur desires, but the desires of human nature, the gift of giving back. To be a successful entrepreneur, it is important to not only make money, and create a wealth of success for yourself and your company, it is also important to make a name for yourself outside your business success. Touching the lives of others, personally, will leave a more impactful legacy in the long run.

So why create a legacy? Why go through all of this trouble just to "make a name for yourself?" Well, as legacy was previously defined, you not only make a name for yourself, but you are passing on something of great use onto generations, and generations to come. Something that you have devised, created, prepared and will be able to help those after you. A positive stamp on this world.

Leaving a legacy means you made it in the business world, and if you are lucky enough to be as remarkable as Bill Gates, you made it in the philanthropic world as well. Leaving a legacy means you took that chance, that risk, that road less traveled. Ordinary people fear change, fear something new, fear the unknown. For those brave enough to embrace it and succeed, you become a leader, and will then leave a legacy.

So consider your path, your "legacy". What will you leave behind? Will it be a journey, a story, or a path of righteousness? The choice is yours. Remember this: Success can be defined by many terms; wealth, money, power, management. However, to leave a legacy you have to not only have succeeded as an entrepreneur, but you have to have mattered to people as well.

I am personally leaving you with this book. My hope is that it is has given you golden nuggets that you can carry with you throughout your journey in this life, and as an entrepreneur.

I once heard a quote that stuck with me: "When you know better, you do better". You now have been equipped with the type of valuable information that many people have attended business courses to receive. It is all included in this manual that you'll be able to refer back to as you deem necessary.

You are now empowered. You've educated yourself. You understand your why is you. You're not going to let your fears surpass you. You my friend are an unstoppable entrepreneur.

Here is to your success!

ABOUT THE AUTHOR

Daniel Desta is an award winning, nationally recognized, business coach, director of lending, and entrepreneur with over a decade of experience. Google has recognized his as an expert in the small business lending field, and he is known amongst his clients as being highly knowledgeable, credible, and a leader in his industry. At the age of 21, Daniel became the partner of a prestigious firm, and led a team of 17 agents to success.

He saw great success early on, as well as great failure, but didn't allow that to stop him. From tackling all of his personal fears, choosing to live authentically, developing a solid brand, and identifying his "Why", Daniel bounced back from a life changing fall. Armed with experience, he made it his latest offering of The Entrepreneur's Handbook.

Daniel's guiding principle in all his endeavors is, "Where there is a will, there is always a way", and he strives to help others see their own personal will--- and way. His latest offering allows Daniel to work every day fulfilling his passion for entrepreneurship, but also allows him to share that passion with other entrepreneurs.

In the process---making a monumental impact on their lives.